Silly Nomads

Volume 2 Teacher's Guide

Silly Nomads Go Ninja Crazy

Written in collaboration with Progressive Bridges, Inc.
©2017 Mohalland Lewis LLC

© 2017 Mohalland Lewis, LLC
All rights reserved.

© 2015 Document Text
Written in collaboration with
Progressive Bridges, Inc., Naples, FL

Published in the United States by
Mohalland Lewis, LLC

Cover Illustration by Kate Santee

No part of this book may be reproduced, scanned, stored in a retrieval system,
or transmitted by any means without the written permission of
Mohalland Lewis, LLC.

ISBN 978-0-9990303-1-8

This lesson plan is suitable for use with students in Grades 3-5. All activities are aligned with the ELA Common Core State Standards (CCSS) for Reading, Writing, and Speaking & Listening. Activities can be modified as needed based on specific needs and ability levels within those standards.

Learning Objectives:

1. Identify characteristics of ninja warriors.
2. Explain and give examples of real and imaginary story events.
3. Compare and contrast characters and settings with one's own life experiences.
4. Engage in using the imagination to create new adventures and expand ideas and possibilities.
5. Utilize and grow literacy skills through story interaction.

This story supports the following beliefs:

- Education is valuable to personal success in life.
- New knowledge can fuel imagination.
- Using your imagination is a fun, inexpensive, and powerful experience.
- Entertainment and happiness can be found without a lot of material possessions.

Note to the Teacher:

Use this lesson plan as a flexible guide to support **Silly Nomads – Volume 2** with a variety of options from which to choose based on your students' interests and ability levels. All activities are aligned with the ELA Common Core State Standards (CCSS) to ensure quality, relevance, and rigor in the academic classroom. Best practice pages for instructional vocabulary activities and read-a-loud strategies are listed on pages 31-33 of this lesson plan document.

A Lesson Guide for Teachers

- **This lesson plan** provides educators with several activity menus that include a range of specific reading skill activities and open-ended questions, aligned with Common Core State Standards (CCSS), enabling students to create meaningful connections to story characters and events as they enhance critical thinking, reading, writing, speaking, and listening skills.

- **This lesson plan** provides educators with cross-curriculum activities to reinforce concepts in social studies, geography, math, science, and the arts, as well as in the area of literacy. Look for specific icons for these connections.

- **This lesson plan** provides educators with a menu of engaging activities for elementary students designed to help them extend their learning by encouraging imaginative and innovative ideas, much like the story characters. Many activities also involve research-related skills designed to appeal to 21st Century learners as they explore a variety of concepts and possible career interests. These activities can be easily modified or adapted for children of many ages, maturity levels, and academic ability levels.

A Home Connection for Students and Parents

- **This lesson plan** provides teachers with learning activities and discussion prompts for students to share with their parents at home to reinforce learning concepts, promote literacy in families, and to provide ways to keep parents connected to the classroom.

 Home Connection Activity

Assessments to Check for Understanding

- **This lesson plan** provides teachers with several assessments to measure student understanding of the story. A Pre and Post Assessment given at the beginning and end of the book provide evidence of concept learning throughout the story. A short 10 question quiz is part of every lesson and measures student comprehension of the part of the book covered for that specific lesson. While most questions are multiple choice or true/false, quizzes do contain a few open-ended responses. A final Reading Comprehension Assessment provides an open-ended response assessment to measure further story comprehension.

Silly Nomads Go Ninja Crazy

Lesson #1   Chapters 1-3   Pages 1-32

Lesson Focus: The idea of a mission is introduced by main characters, Suhcrom and Naddih. The boys start their Ninja training with an obstacle course and a weight lifting experiment.

Basic Story Vocabulary   (2-5, Reading – Standard 4)

strutted	mission	pleading	obstacle course
endurance	piercing	ferocious	prickles
quivered	clutched	clamped	curfew
trance	pledge	brim	biceps
peered	restless	rummage	scampered

Pre-teach vocabulary to introduce students to new words prior to reading the chapter. Choose an *Instructional Vocabulary Activity* from page 31.

Reading the Text

Silly Nomads books make fun read-aloud experiences for students. Varying these strategies reinforces interaction with text and creates ongoing interest for students. Choose a *Read-Aloud Strategy* from page 32-33 for in-class reading.

Facilitated Discussion Prompts

👀 Discuss as a group: When the author wrote, "The boys looked at each other. No words were necessary." (p. 10), what do you think the boys were thinking? Why were no words necessary? (2-5, Speaking & Listening – Standards 1, 2, & 6)

👀 As a group, discuss what it means to "spill the beans". (2-5, Speaking & Listening – Standards 1, 2, & 6)

👀 Predict, discuss and make a strong inference about what would happen to the boys if they broke their curfew. (2-5, Speaking & Listening – Standards 1, 2, & 6)

👀 When Naddih told Suhcrom to look in a certain direction and calls it "two o'clock", what does he mean? Discuss different ways of describing a location. (2-5, Speaking & Listening – Standards 1, 2, & 6)

👀 What does it mean to "get something off your chest"? Discuss what kinds of things people like to "get off their chest". (2-5, Speaking & Listening – Standards 1, 2, & 6)

Reading Comprehension Activities

👀 Create a timeline of 5 – 8 events for this section of the book. (2-5, Reading – Standard 2)

👀 Describe how Suhcrom and Naddih measured the amount of time they could lift weights. Make a list of the different ways they could have measured this. (2-5, Reading – Standards 1, 2, & 4)

👀 If you were a Ninja in training, how would you get into shape? Use clues from the story to explain how you would get into shape to be a top notch ninja. (2-5, Reading – Standards 1, 2, & 4)

👀 Create an interactive vocabulary list and game using Kahoot (www.Kahoot.com) and share it with the class. (2-5, Reading – Standard 4)

Writing Prompts

What is the difference between "complaining" and "speaking your mind"? Write 3 paragraphs to explain the difference between these two words and provide at least one example of each word. (2-5, Writing - Standards 3, 5, & 6)

The boys believe that running an obstacle course every day will improve their ninja strength and endurance. In a paragraph, explain at least 3 ways an obstacle course will help them. (2-5, Writing – Standard 1)

Pretend you are one of the boys. Write a letter to Jomfeh convincing him to let you stay out after your set curfew. (2-5, Writing – Standard 1; 2-5, Speaking & Listening – Standard 1, 2, & 6)

Write a paragraph describing the ultimate ninja, the size of biceps, his/her moves, and skills. (2-5, Writing – Standard 2)

Curriculum Connections

 **Measuring Movement**

Time yourself doing an exercise with a partner. How many different ways can you think of to measure time or repetitions? Measure the exercises you and a partner are doing 3 different ways. Create a poster to show what you did. (2-5, Reading – Standards 1 & 2)

 **Count & Graph**

Choose 3 different exercises. Practice these same exercises every day for 2 weeks. Graph your progress daily using either a count or time measure. Graph your progress with a bar graph and a line graph. (2-5, Reading – Standards 1, 2, and 6)

 Fitness Plan

Research how to improve physical strength through nutrition and fitness. Create a fitness plan for a month based on your findings. Make a schedule showing exactly what to eat and what exercises to do to build strength. (2-5, Reading – Standards 1 & 2)

 Mission

Do you have a solution to getting past Sticky Fingers to retrieve the book? Create a mission to retrieve the book. Lay out your plan in numbered steps. Include a map or diagram of your plan. (2-5, Reading – Standards 1 & 2)

 Act It Out

Use the verbs from the vocabulary list and practice acting out each of the verbs. Have a contest among the class to see who can act out the meaning of the word the best. Vote with hand clap volume after each contestant has had a turn to act out the word. (2-5, Reading – Standards 1 & 2)

Research & Imagination Activities

 Design an Obstacle Course

Research various obstacle courses to get some ideas of the kinds of activities they involve. Plot a full obstacle course for you and your friends using materials you can find around your house. After the course has been created, take pictures of you and your friends running the course. (2-5, Writing – Standards 2, 6, 7, & 8; 2-5, Reading – Standard 9)

 Ninja Jump Competition

Create 5 new Ninja-style jumps using a ramp. Describe each jump step by step using captions and diagrams on a poster. Video yourself and a friend performing these Ninja jumps and share it with your class. Involve your class in rating your performance on each jump on a scale of 1 – 10. (2-5, Writing – Standards 2, 6, 7, & 8)

 **Obstacle Course Map**

Imagine you and a friend are the main characters in the story. Research more about the materials the boys may have available to them in Jamaica. Imagine how they might add to their obstacle course beyond their weight lifting and ramp. Create a map (either 3D or flat) of the obstacle course they might design. (2-5, Writing – Standards 2, 6, 7, & 8; 2-5, Reading – Standard 9)

  **Physical Exercise Career**

Imagine a career involving physical exercise. Research 3 careers that relate to physical exercise. For each career, make a list of 3 interesting facts about it. Place a star next to the career you like most. (2-5, Writing – Standards 2, 6 &7; 2-5, Reading – Standards 3 & 5)

Silly Nomads Go Ninja Crazy - Volume 2

Lesson #1   Home Connection Activities

🏠 Create an obstacle course in your yard or neighborhood with whatever materials you have available to you. Open the course to your friends and neighbors to use. Take a picture or video of the course and share it with your class.

🏠 Read a book about Ninja training. Make a list of all of the training being a serious Ninja requires.

🏠 Create your own makeshift Ninja outfit. Draw a picture of your customized Ninja outfit.

🏠 Help Jomfeh by creating a list of possible consequences for Suhcrom and Naddih in case they miss their curfew.

WE CONNECTED!

My favorite character in this part of the story was _____

because he/she _____

I liked the part in the story when _____

_____

I circled the house beside of the activity we completed.

Student: _____ Date: _____

Parent(s): _____ Date: _____

This page may be copied for student/parent use.

13

Silly Nomads Go Ninja Crazy

Lesson #2   Chapters 4-6   Pages 33-62

Lesson Focus: The Silly Nomads Ninjas create their ninja tools, survive a pop quiz, and experience an unforgettable roof top adventure.

Basic Story Vocabulary   (2-5, Reading – Standard 4)

ninja stars	despicable	arrogance	knight
boomerang	carve	arthritis	commotion
curiosity	naught	makeshift	limply
mercy	nestled	intruders	
slay	stimulating	democratic process	

Pre-teach vocabulary to introduce students to new words prior to reading the chapter. Choose an *Instructional Vocabulary Activity* from page 31.

Reading the Text

Silly Nomads books make fun read-aloud experiences for students. Varying these strategies reinforces interaction with text and creates ongoing interest for students. Choose a *Read-Aloud Strategy* from page 32-33 for in-class reading.

Facilitated Discussion Prompts

👀 How did the authors' use of a memory increase your understanding of what Suhcrom was feeling inside? (2-5, Speaking & Listening – Standards 1, 2, & 6)

👀 Have you ever tried to make something out of wood? Compare your experience with that of the boys. (2-5, Speaking & Listening – Standards 1, 2, & 6)

👀 Give examples that illustrate how Naddih is curious. Can you think of any other characters in other books you have read who are also curious? (2-5, Speaking & Listening – Standards 1, 2, & 6)

👀 How does "knighting" themselves help the boys feel brave? (2-5, Speaking & Listening – Standards 1, 2, & 6)

👀 How do you think the boys will finally get Suhcrom's book back? Make a prediction and explain your thinking. (2-5, Speaking & Listening – Standards 1, 2, & 6)

Reading Comprehension

👀 Explain the difference between "stimulating" and "dangerous". Divide a piece of blank white paper in half. On one side, write "stimulating" and on the other write "dangerous". Include words in each area to describe the meaning of the word. Illustrate an example of each word from the story so far. (2-5, Reading – Standard 2)

👀 What have you learned about Suhcrom and Naddih in this part of the book? How are they similar? How are they different? Create a picture of each character and place descriptive words around the appropriate character to illustrate your thoughts. (2-5, Reading – Standards 1, 2, & 4)

👀 Recall the order of events in this part of the book. Retell them through the creation of a comic strip or video slides (flip pages of a sequence of pictures and sentences retelling the story as you retell it out loud on a video). (2-5, Reading – Standards 1, 2, & 4)

👀 Create an interactive vocabulary list and game using Kahoot (www.Kahoot.com) and share it with the class. (2-5, Reading – Standard 4)

Writing Prompts

👀💡 Imagine the conversation of the villagers about the mysterious footsteps on their roofs. Write a conversation using quotation marks about what you think they may have said to each other. (2-5, Writing – Standards 3, 5, & 6)

👀💡 Imagine that you are Naddih. Write an email from Naddih to Suhcrom about their current adventure. Be sure to try to write it with words, phrases, and his "voice". (2-5, Writing – Standards 1 & 2)

👀💡 Predict what might have happened if Naddih had not been able to pull Suhcrom back up on the roof. Rewrite the next events the way you think they may have happened. (2-5, Writing – Standard 1; 2-5, Speaking & Listening – Standards 1, 2, & 6)

👀💡 Write a memory flash of a memory you have from when you were younger. (2-5, Writing – Standard 1)

Curriculum Connections

 **New Ninja Story Map**
Create a new Silly Nomads ninja adventure that takes place in another country. Research the story location and create a story board of main story events. (2-5, Reading – Standard 1)

 **Mission Map**
Create a mission map of the boys' adventure in Chapter 6. (2-5, Reading – Standards 1, 2, and 6)

 **Knighting**
The custom of "knighting" is interesting. Research this custom and create 3 slides to tell more about it. (2-5, Reading – Standards 1 & 2)

 Class Spelling Bee
Use the vocabulary words from this lesson to have a class spelling bee. (2-5, Reading – Standard 4)

 Ninja Weapon Advertisement
Research more about one of the following Ninja weapons: boomerang, Ninja throwing stars, sword. Create an advertisement for the weapon you researched and include these facts in your advertisement. (2-5, Reading – Standards 1 & 2)

 **Help Suhcrom with Spelling**
Suhcrom wants to beat the girls in spelling. Create a study plan for Suhcrom to help him improve his spelling skills once he gets his book back from Hamburg. Be sure to include a schedule and strategies to help him keep focused. (2-5, Writing – Standards 2, 6, 7, & 8)

 **Create & Give a Pop Quiz**
Jomfeh liked to quiz the boys to be sure they were reading. Imagine you are Jomfeh. Think of a chapter you just studied. Create a 5-question pop quiz for someone in your class to take. Be sure to create an answer key. Trade quizzes with another classmate and check each other's answers. (2-5, Writing – Standards 1, 2, & 3)

Research & Imagination Activities

 **Research & Design a Ninja Star**

Imagine that you are in a Ninja star-throwing competition. Research the best throwing stars and design one you think could win the competition. (2-5, Writing – Standards 2, 6, 7, & 8; 2-5, Reading – Standard 9)

 **Imagine Being a Reporter…**

Imagine you are a reporter covering the mysterious "footsteps on the roof" story in the neighborhood of Palmerston Close for the evening news. Create a makeshift microphone and interview at least 3 villagers. Write at least 3 questions on index cards in advance to use in the interviews. If available, ask someone to video your production. (2-5, Writing – Standards 2, 6, 7, & 8; 2-5, Reading – Standard 9)

 **Research Military Jobs**

Army Rangers, Navy Seals, and Marines all go on missions as part of their jobs. Research 1 branch of the military and create a 4- slide power point explaining 1) what their jobs are like, 2) a few reasons their jobs might interest you, and 3) how you can prepare to go into their jobs someday. Share it with your class. (2-5, Writing – Standards 2, 6, 7, & 8; 2-5, Reading – Standard 9; 2-5, Speaking & Listening – Standards 1, 2, & 6)

 **Research Woodworking Jobs**

Learn more about various woodworking jobs, such a cabinet-making, carpentry, construction, and deck-building. Create a poster about 1 woodworking career describing the job skills they need to develop to be good at it. (2-5, Writing – Standards 2, 6, 7, & 8; 2-5, Reading – Standard 9)

Silly Nomads Go Ninja Crazy - Volume 2

Lesson #2   Home Connection Activities

🏠 As you stand at the front door of your home looking outside, draw and describe what you see at 1 o'clock, 3 o'clock, and 5 o'clock.

🏠 Write an email to a good friend to get something "off your chest". Notice how it feels to share that with a trusted friend.

🏠 Plan a mission that you and a good friend can experience and complete together. What is the purpose of the mission? What mnaterials will you need to bring to accomplish it? Record this to share in class later.

🏠 Play a game of dominoes with a friend. Afterwards, make up your own version of dominoes. Write down the rules and how to play the game step by step.

WE CONNECTED!

My favorite character in this part of the story was _____

because he/she _____

I liked the part in the story when _____

_____

I circled the house beside of the activity we completed.

Student: _____   Date: _____

Parent(s): _____   Date: _____

This page may be copied for student/parent use.

Silly Nomads Go Ninja Crazy

Lesson #3   Chapters 7-9   Pages 63-95

Lesson Focus: Suhcrom and Naddih enjoy an afternoon of chaos in the family TV room and take a final mission to get back Suhcrom's beloved book.

Basic Story Vocabulary   (2-5, Reading – Standard 4)

guide	vendors	scaled	hightailed
landmark	jerk	gully	crevice
rubbish	comrades	embankment	cricket
brawl	stratification	bearings	dominoes
chaos	tandem	chatter	adrenaline

Pre-teach vocabulary to introduce students to new words prior to reading the chapter. Choose an *Instructional Vocabulary Activity* from page 31.

Reading the Text

Silly Nomad books make fun read-aloud experiences for students. Varying these strategies reinforces interaction with text and creates ongoing interest for students. Choose a *Read-Aloud Strategy* from page 32-33 for in-class reading.

Facilitated Discussion Prompts

Tell about a funny experience when someone you know fell asleep while watching TV. (2-5, Speaking & Listening – Standards 1, 2, & 6)

Why did Naddih carry so much in his backpack? Have you seen other kids do the same thing? (2-5, Speaking & Listening – Standards 1, 2, & 6)

👀　At the end of the story, what do you think Naddih sees that encourages him to forgive Suhcrom for leaving him and jump up to complete his mission of dressing Sticky Fingers? Do you predict this will play a part in the next Silly Nomads book? Why or why not? (2-5, Speaking & Listening – Standards 1, 2, & 6)

👀　Have you ever had a pillow fight like the boys did in front of the TV? What do you think makes this kind of chaos so exhilarating and fun? Describe your experience. (2-5, Speaking & Listening – Standards 1, 2, & 6)

👀　Describe the scene where Hamburg's mom embarrassed Naddih in front of the entire village. How do you think Naddih felt? Do you think it will keep him from doing it again? Why or why not? (2-5, Speaking & Listening – Standards 1, 2, & 6)

Reading Comprehension Activities

👀　Imagine you are one of the boys in the story. Make up a new adventure having to do with Sticky Fingers, the dog. Create a mini-book of your adventure. (2-5, Reading – Standard 2)

👀　Reread House Rules (chapter 8) and pay special attention to the dialogue between the boys in front of the TV. It is easy to understand that they are good friends who spend a lot of time together because of the way they talk with each other. Think about how you and your friends interact as a group. Create a conversation between you and several of your friends that shows how well you know each other. (2-5, Reading – Standards 1, 2, & 4)

👀　Humor can be difficult to show in a story. Choose one humorous scene from these 3 chapters and describe in your own words what made it funny to you. What did the authors do in their writing to illustrate the humor so well? Create a cartoon retelling the humorous scene in your own words. (2-5, Reading – Standards 1, 2, & 4)

👀 Re-enact one of the scenes in this section of the book. Capture the re-enactment in digital pictures. Use the pictures in a presentation format (power point, movie trailer, digital story, etc.) to share it with the class. As a class, vote on the re-enactments that are most like the actual story event. (2-5, Reading – Standards 1, 2, & 4)

👀 Create an interactive vocabulary list and game using Kahoot (www.Kahoot.com) and share it with the class. (2-5, Reading – Standard 4)

Writing Prompts

👀💡 Create a jerk recipe of your own. Be sure to list ingredients and write out the steps carefully. (2-5, Writing – Standards 3, 5, & 6)

👀💡 Write a paragraph to describe the change in Hamburg's mom in chapter 9. Explain why you think she changed her feelings toward Naddih. (2-5, Writing – Standard 1)

👀💡 What did the boys learn in chapter 9? How do you think these learned lessons will impact their future lessons? (2-5, Writing – Standard 1; 2-5, Speaking & Listening – Standard 1, 2, & 6)

👀💡 Write about a time when you had to choose between getting in trouble with someone or allowing the other person to take the blame. What did you do and why? Would you choose differently if you were able to do it over? Why or why not? (2-5, Writing – Standard 1)

👀💡 Which of the brothers do you believe is the most competitive? Support your answers with examples. (2-5, Writing – Standard 2)

Curriculum Connections

   Create a Map with Landmarks

Track the boys' run home in chapter 7. Create a map tracing their journey. Draw and label the landmarks along the track. Mark the boys' paths in red. (2-5, Reading – Standards 1 & 2)

  House Rule Comparison

Compare and contrast Suhcrom and Naddih's house rules with the rules at your house. (2-5, Reading – Standards 1, 2, and 6)

   **Cook Jamaican Style**

Research a variety of spices used in Jamaican cooking, such as curry and jerk. With the help of an adult, prepare cooked bite-sized pieces of chicken, each in a different spice, and skewer the pieces on a toothpick. Serve in class as a tasting experiment. Graph likes and dislikes of the different spices. (2-5, Reading – Standards 1, 2, & 6)

   **Color TV Timeline**

Research the invention and availability of the color TV. When and where did this take place and how did it evolve? Create a timeline to illustrate the history of the color TV. (2-5, Reading – Standards 1, 2, & 6)

 **Antenna Drawing**

One of the kids commented that Naddih had to be the antenna with their old black and white TV. Why do you think Naddih was used as an antenna? Research more to find out how Naddih could have been an antenna. Draw and label an illustration to show what you learn. (2-5, Reading – Standards 1, 2, & 6)

Research & Imagination Activities

 **Create a New Game**

Research the games of dominoes and cricket, common games played in Jamaica. Decide which game you like best and design a new game using either dominoes or cricket equipment. Create a poster with the game name, pictures, and rules. (2-5, Writing – Standards 2, 6, 7, & 8; 2-5, Reading – Standard 9)

 **Your Run**

Imagine that you are running from your school to your home. Map out the route. Place landmarks along the route. Label the landmarks. (2-5, Writing – Standards 2)

 **Design a Backpack**

Pretend you are Naddih with a lot of items to carry with you to school. Design a new backpack to carry items needed for a number of destinations. For example, you could design a special backpack just for going to the grocery store or for going to the mall with friends. (2-5, Writing – Standards 2, 6, 7, & 8; 2-5, Reading – Standard 9)

 **Build a Model**

Research more about Palmerston Close (a neighborhood in the town of Portsmouth) and life in Jamaica. Build a model of what you imagine the town to be like based on this book. (2-5, Reading – Standards 1 & 2)

 **Persistence**

Toward the end of the story, Naddih did not give up having adventures, even when things weren't going well and he felt alone. Persistence is a character strength that describes someone who never gives up. Interview 3 people who have jobs and ask them how persistence helps them to be successful in their jobs. Collect their responses and create a poster about persistence at work to share with your class. (2-5, Speaking & Listening – Standards 1, 2, & 6; 2-5, Writing – Standards 1 & 2)

 **Planning Skills**

Suhcrom planned the boys' missions in advance and was careful to write it down on paper. The skill of planning ahead is important in many jobs. Research some jobs that require good planning skills. Print or draw pictures to illustrate at least 5 of these jobs and use them to create a collage. In the middle of the collage, place the words, "Planning Skills Needed", and hang it in the classroom. (2-5, Reading – Standards 1 & 6)

Silly Nomads Go Ninja Crazy - Volume 2

Lesson #3   Home Connection Activities

🏠 Have a "pillow fight" (with parent permission) with your friends or siblings. Draw a picture of the chaos!

🏠 A landmark is a location of special significance or something memorable. Find a special landmark in your town. Take a picture of it and explain the landmark's history or significance to the class.

🏠 Take an inventory of your backpack. Make a list of everything you carry in it and why each item is important to you. If you are able, weigh each item to see how heavy your backpack is each day!

🏠 Think of a time when you were persistent even when you may have felt like giving up. Create a paper slide video (Google this) or a cartoon about the experience and share it with the class.

WE CONNECTED!

My favorite character in this part of the story was _____

because he/she _____

I liked the part in the story when _____

_____

I circled the house beside of the activity we completed.

Student: _____ Date: _____

Parent(s): _____ Date: _____

This page may be copied for student/parent use.

Instructional Vocabulary Activities

(2-5, Reading – Standard 4)

Frayer Diagram: Divide the paper into fourths. Write a vocabulary word in the center (or the intersection of both lines). In one corner, place your own definition of the word. In the second corner, place facts or characteristics of the vocabulary word, and in the third, place examples of the word, and in the fourth, place non-examples of the word.
http://www.longwood.edu/staff/jonescd/projects/educ530/aboxley/graphicorg/fraym.htm

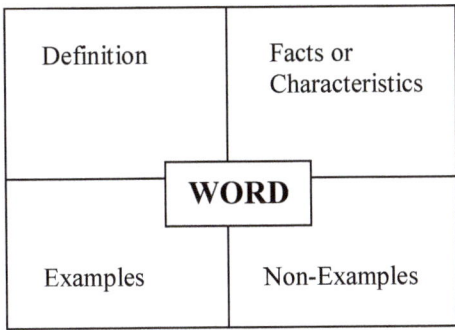

Word Sorts: Organize all of the vocabulary words into groupings that have common characteristics. Make up as many grouping titles as needed to go with the groupings. To vary the activity, sort the words by character association (which words are best associated with which story character), a great pre and post reading activity.

Add Words to an Interactive Word Wall: Include every new vocabulary word introduced on an interactive word wall. Interactive word walls are comprised of a wall or classroom space, wall, door, bulletin board, divider, etc. which is designated for these new words. Words are printed or created and then placed on the wall for frequent student use through discussion, writing, review, reading, grouping, illustration, or manipulation throughout classroom activities. The more the words are used following introduction, the more effective and interactive the Word Wall becomes for students.

Read-Aloud Strategies

(2-5, Speaking & Listening – Standards 1 & 2; 2-5, Reading – Standard 4)

Buddy Reading: Place students into pairs prior to reading. Students take turns reading out loud to each other, each a page or paragraph at a time.

Popcorn Reading (after Silent Pre-Reading): After an initial silent reading of the passage, one person begins to read the passage aloud. As soon as he/she stops reading, another student "pops" in to continue where the previous student stopped reading. It is helpful to set ground rules at the beginning of this activity, such as a maximum or minimum number of sentences or words read. This activity reinforces attention to print, listening, and collaboration as the object is to complete a passage in a smooth manner. It is important to allow the students to take the initiative to read rather than calling on them.

Jigsaw Reading: Jigsaw reading is helpful for use with longer passages or multiple passages of related text content. Split the passage(s) into sections and assign each section to a group of students so that every group reads a different part of the entire passage. The groups work together to read and understand their assigned passage. Their responsibility is to return to the whole group to summarize and/or teach them the content of their assigned passage. As a variation, allow the groups choices in how they teach the content to the entire group.

Choral Reading: Choral reading can be accomplished several different ways. It can include an initial silent read, and preplanning of how the passage can be most effectively read together. Choose parts of the passage to be read chorally, all students reading aloud together, and parts to be read aloud by one person or several different people. Commonly, the specific parts you want students to recall are those selected for choral reading. Choral reading can be fun as well as support and encourage listening skills and active engagement.

Read with Main Idea or Timeline Maps/Advanced Organizers: Main idea maps are a type of advanced organizer that effectively supports students in getting meaning from passages. A skeleton main idea map is most helpful in starting students with this strategy. Provide a web or diagram showing the main idea of the passage, as well as designated blank areas for the main points supporting the main idea that are connected to the main idea. Students read the passage aloud or silently and complete the map with the main points, as well as minor detail supporting those main points. This can be accomplished collectively out loud or as individuals in silence. In time, students can move to creating their own mind maps of passages. Use SmartArt in Microsoft Word for templates.

Oral Reading with CLOZE: For younger students, the teacher can read the book aloud to a group of students, periodically pausing for students to complete the appropriate word in text based on listening comprehension, syntax, and language skills.

Live Theatre Reading: After an initial reading of the passage, allow students to take different character roles within the story and read it as a play. The narrator reads any parts not in direct quotations. This interactive reading, especially when done in small groups, allows students to practice reading skills while they pay close attention to quotation marks, conversation between characters, and listening skills.

ASSESSMENTS

Pre and Post Assessments, Quizzes, and
Reading Comprehension Assessments
may be copied for student use.

Silly Nomads Go Ninja Crazy - Volume 2
Pre and Post Assessment

Place T (truth) or M (myth) by each statement.

Pre	Statement	Post
	Landmarks are helpful in navigating a journey.	
	Cricket is a game played with a ball, while dominoes are played with tiles.	
	A heavy backpack is a sign of a good student.	
	Color TV's have been common in most homes around the world since 1950.	
	Knighting someone makes him braver.	
	Running an obstacle course and lifting weights builds strength and endurance.	
	Ninjas are strong and agile.	
	Ninja stars and boomerangs work the same way.	
	Carving something out of wood is a slow process.	
	Jerk is a type of candy.	
	Reading is important for success in life.	
	An obstacle course is simple to construct.	

Silly Nomads Go Ninja Crazy - Volume 2
Pre and Post Assessment

Answer Key

Pre	Statement	Post
T	Landmarks are helpful in navigating a journey.	
T	Cricket is a game played with a ball, while dominoes are played with tiles.	
M	A heavy backpack is a sign of a good student.	
M	Color TV's have been common in most homes around the world since 1950.	
M	Knighting someone makes him braver.	
T	Running an obstacle course and lifting weights builds strength and endurance.	
T	Ninjas are strong and agile.	
M	Ninja stars and boomerangs work the same way.	
T	Carving something out of wood is a slow process.	
M	Jerk is a type of candy.	
T	Reading is important for success in life.	
T	An obstacle course is simple to construct.	

Silly Nomads Go Ninja Crazy - Volume 2

Lesson #1 Quiz   Chapters 1-3

1. When does Suhcrom hiccup?
   a. When he is laughing
   b. When he is nervous
   c. When he eats too fast

2. Which word do the boys use to describe ninja training on an obstacle course?
   a. Endurance
   b. Weapons training
   c. Stealth

3. Mr. Broomie was
   a. An imaginary ghost
   b. The neighbor
   c. A mean dog

4. Why didn't Suhcrom want anyone else to know they were pretending to be ninjas on a mission?
   a. To avoid getting in trouble
   b. To avoid being laughed at
   c. To avoid having to share the obstacle course

5. The watch the boys discovered is described as
   a. A piece of junk
   b. A broken watch
   c. A valuable thing

6. What is the most important thing Suhcrom stressed about ninjas?
   a. They jump very high.
   b. They must land on their big toes.
   c. They are completely quiet.

7. When Jomfeh tells the boys to soccer some books, what does he mean?
   a. They should read books rather than play.
   b. They should kick books around the yard.
   c. They should chase books rather than soccer balls.

8. We can infer that Jomfeh
   a. Dances with books.
   b. Values books and reading.
   c. Believes playing is important.

9. The phrase "smell of fishy sea water" reminds us that the boys live
   a. Near a pond.
   b. On an island.
   c. Near someone cooking fish.

10. We can infer that the boys' mama
    a. Thought their older hut was much like a castle.
    b. Liked their older hut with the muddy yard better than where they were currently living.
    c. Did not have much money when she could only afford the hut with the muddy yard.

Silly Nomads Go Ninja Crazy - Volume 2

Lesson #2 Quiz   Chapters 4-6

1. Why wouldn't the boys try to get the throwing star off of Mr. Broomie's roof?
   a. It was too high.
   b. They were afraid of Mr. Broomie.
   c. They knew they could make another one out of wood.

2. How much ice cream money did Suhcrom have to give up when he broke the car window?
   a. $50
   b. We can't tell.
   c. $80

3. How did the boys whittle the wooden ninja star?
   a. With Jomfeh's knife
   b. With a kitchen knife
   c. With a nail clipper knife

4. How could you tell Suhcrom was nervous and frustrated with his spelling performance?
   a. He had sweaty palms.
   b. He had the hiccups.
   c. Both a and b

5. How would you describe Suhcrom?
   a. Timid & shy
   b. Competitive & bossy
   c. Smart & curious

6. How would you describe Naddih?
   a. Lazy & sleepy
   b. Curious & energetic
   c. Negative & cautious

7. Why did the boys decide to knight each other?
   a. So they would become brave enough to jump on the roofs in completing their mission.
   b. So they would pretend they were protecting a castle.
   c. So they could pretend they were sword fighting for the kingdom.

8. Why did Suhcrom listen to Naddih's crazy ideas?
   a. Because he thought they sounded fun.
   b. Because he wanted to prove they were actually his ideas.
   c. Because he wanted to show his bravery after being knighted.

9. Suhcrom's nervousness was based on his past experience when he was
   a. Flying a kite from a roof
   b. Watching cartoons on the roof
   c. Almost fell from a roof

10. What ran through Suhcrom's head as he was hanging off the roof?
    a. How he wanted to beat Enomih in spelling someday.
    b. How he wanted to get back at Naddih for making him do this.
    c. How he wanted to fulfill his promise to send money to Ethiopia.

Silly Nomads Go Ninja Crazy - Volume 2

Lesson #3 Quiz   Chapters 7-9

1. Why did Naddih have a difficult time running home?
    a. He didn't want to watch cartoons.
    b. His backpack was too heavy.
    c. He was out of shape.

2. What was Naddih concerned about in jumping the crevice on the run home?
    a. Broken glass, rocks, and smelly trash
    b. Water depth and hidden rocks
    c. His short legs

3. What was the ultimate mission?
    a. Dress Sticky Fingers
    b. Get Suhcrom's book back
    c. Get Suhcrom's book back and dress Sticky Fingers

4. Why did Naddih go over the house rules if their friends already knew them?
    a. He liked to remind them.
    b. Jomfeh told him to do it.
    c. Someone always broke them.

5. Why was the TV precious to the boys?
    a. It was a big screen TV.
    b. It was the only color TV in the town.
    c. They had snacks for everyone as they watched.

6. What can we infer about the TV?
   a. They had save money for a long time in order to buy it.
   b. Most people in town had a color TV also.
   c. They kept it on all day and evening.

7. Why do you think the boys describe Suhcrom's book as magical and treasured?
   a. Because it has special imaginary adventure ideas in it.
   b. Because words jump from it into the mind.
   c. Because they know it holds knowledge they need to be successful.

8. Why did Suhcrom leave Naddih behind during the mission?
   a. He knew it was too late to save him.
   b. He figured he had earned it since he couldn't keep quiet.
   c. He wanted him to get into trouble.

9. How did Hamburg's mother punish Naddih?
   a. She gave him a time out.
   b. She called his father.
   c. She embarrassed him in front of the neighbors.

10. What part of the mission did Naddih complete on his own?
    a. He got the book back.
    b. He met Mr. Broomie.
    c. He dressed Hamburg's dog.

Silly Nomads Go Ninja Crazy - Volume 2

Quiz Answer Key

Question	Lesson 1 Quiz	Lesson 2 Quiz	Lesson 3 Quiz
1	B	B	B
2	A	B	A
3	B	C	C
4	B	C	C
5	C	B	B
6	C	B	A
7	A	A	C
8	B	C	A
9	B	A	C
10	A	C	C

Silly Nomads Go Ninja Crazy - Volume 2

Reading Comprehension Assessment

1. Compare and contrast Suhcrom and Naddih. Use a Venn Diagram or a T-chart to share your thoughts.

2. Do you think Suhcrom will become a good student now that he has his book back? Why or why not?

3. What do you think Naddih is feeling when he says, "It's happening again!"?

4. What do you predict the next book will be about? Why?

5. What do you think Naddih saw on the wall of his bedroom the night he got caught by Hamburg's mom?

Silly Nomads

Look for these other Silly Nomads adventures!

Volume 1 – Silly Nomads From Palmerston Close

Volume 3 – Silly Nomads Jubilee Bike Race Heroes

Volume 4 – Coming Soon

www.ingramcontent.com/pod-product-compliance
Lightning Source LLC
Chambersburg PA
CBHW040912020526
44116CB00026B/36